The WORD of GOD

... with a TWIST

The
WORD
of
GOD

... *with a*

FATHER LARRY HEHMAN

BUTLER BOOKS

ISBN 978-1-941953-80-8
Printed in the United States of America

Published by
BUTLER BOOKS
P.O. Box 7311
Louisville, KY 40257
phone: (502) 897-9393
fax: (502) 897-9797
www.butlerbooks.com

ABOUT THE AUTHOR

Fr. Larry Hehman, MA, MEd, was ordained a Roman Catholic Priest in Innsbruck, Austria, in 1965. He has served in the Diocese of Covington, Kentucky, and the Diocese of Lexington, Kentucky.

His many years of ministry have afforded him numerous opportunities to serve, including as instructor of German and religion at Covington Latin School (1965–68), chaplain at the University of Kentucky Newman Center (1969–77), first pastor of Holy Spirit Parish at the University of Kentucky Newman Center (1978–86), pastor of Christ the King Church, Lexington, (1986–88), rector of the Cathedral of Christ the King, Lexington (1988–94), founding pastor of Pax Christi Church, Lexington, (1994–2004), priests' personnel director for the Diocese of Lexington (1998–2004), president of the Priests' Senate, Diocese of Covington (1980–92), chair of Presbyterial Council, Diocese of Lexington (1988–90).

Fr. Larry retired in July 2004 and now serves at local parishes where he shares in sacramental, teaching, and preaching ministry. Weekly, since 2013, he has produced a Sunday homily on YouTube. His ministry of preaching the Word has touched the hearts and lives of generations of parishioners in the Bluegrass and far beyond. He is a prophetic voice for social justice issues, the dignity of every person, respect for diversity, and the value of dialogue—with the Word and one another.

CONTENTS

About the Author v

Foreword ix

Introduction xi

180 Gallons of the Best Wine 1

It Is Just the Gardener! But Is It? 5

Pride—The Good Kind 9

Lost and Found—Too Good to Be True? 13

The Unjust Judge 17

What's New? 21

Follow Me 23

The Body and Blood of Christ 27

Badgering God and Dad, Too! 31

Hospitality 35

What Must I Do to Get into Heaven? 39

Am I a Disciple of Jesus? 41

Am I Rich? 43

No Room in the Inn 45

Doubting Thomas and the 51st Anniversary
   of My Priesthood 47

INRI 49

Open, Read, Preach 51

A Leaf 53

Odor of Sanctity 55

Modern Leprosy in Need of a Cure 57

What Is Your Spirituality? 61

The Rest of the Story 63

Plato, Einstein, and Jesus 65
We Are Called to Read and Meditate on Scripture . . . 67
Season Evergreen. 71
Am I Humble? Are You Humble?. 73
If the Church Would Only 77
Are You Saved? 81
Am I a Prophet? 85
Auschwitz vs. the Kingdom of God 89
Cosmic Christ 93
The Messiah, Christos, Jesus 95
Prodigal Son 99
Hurling Stones Is Not Mercy 103
Crashing or Gently, It Is the Spirit 105
Easter Sunday. 107
Suffering 109

Acknowledgments 111

FOREWORD

When I think of Father Larry Hehman, I can't help but be reminded of Jesus' encounter with the apostle Nathaniel. When introduced to Jesus, Nathaniel asks whether anything good can come from Nazareth. Instead of taking offense, Jesus applauded Nathaniel's straightforwardness, saying "there is no deceit in him."

When I arrived as the third Bishop of Lexington, Father Larry was anxious to introduce himself as the first rector of Christ the King, as a cathedral, and the founding pastor of Pax Christi. He lost no time in giving me his assessment of the diocese, my predecessors, and what he thought I should be doing from day one. Perhaps a little taken aback, I have come to apply Jesus' apt description of Nathaniel to Larry, "there is no deceit in him." Father Larry calls them as he sees them. His candor and the freedom with which he offers direction are gifts which I now appreciate.

I have no doubt that it is his direct style, his willingness to get into controversial matters, his familiarity with human flaws and foibles and his practical understanding of what Christian discipleship demands which make Father Larry's homilies accessible and appreciated by many. Not only are his homilies incarnational and down to earth, they are filled with rich insights into the biblical world and the novelty of Jesus who arrives on the scene as Savior, Healer, Brother, Friend, Challenger and, ultimately, as Son of God. Larry invites the listener into that world and helps one to get to know Jesus better.

Father Hehman shares his deep understanding of the Catholic tradition and its theology. His faith and knowledge about that faith was born in what he affectionately calls the "Roman Catholic German Ghetto" of northern Kentucky, nourished in the premiere school of theology in Innsbruck, where Karl Rahner lectured, and is bearing fruit in the Bluegrass where Father Larry not only preaches, but practices this rich teaching.

Sometimes Father Larry's words offend, sometimes they sting, but they always challenge, and they always require further reflection— just like the sermons of the Word Made Flesh. Father Larry has learned to sit with the scriptures, to digest them slowly, and to not miss the humor and sometimes the bizarre that are found in its pages. Above all, Father Larry strives to bring the Word of God alive so that it may transform the hearer and allow him or her to become a more fully engaged member of the Body of Christ.

I hope that you enjoy this collection of homilies. I hope that they provoke further reflection on the scriptures that Father Larry presents. I hope that they lead you to a deeper encounter with the Great Teacher and Preacher, Jesus of Nazareth the Son of God.

+ John Stowe, OFM Conv.
Bishop of Lexington

INTRODUCTION

My sisters and brothers, accept us as we are:
men who like you, need the mercy of God;
poor men, weak, sinful, with faults and limited talents.

Though remaining men and Christians,
we begin to speak the Word of God;
the Word He has sent us to proclaim.
Accept us as the messengers of Christ.
Hear in our human words—
in our fumbling, miserable, and often repetitious words—
the holy, blessed, and powerful Word of God,
the Word that brings God Himself and His eternal life into our midst.

We can only beg you: Pray for us.
Have patience with us.
Carry us.
Accept God's Word and His holy mysteries from us.

—Fr. Karl Rahner SJ

Dear sisters and brothers,

Those words—a prayer, really—were the text I chose for the prayer card shared at my first Mass way back on April 3, 1965. Father Rahner's words moved me, a fresh young priest ready to preach the

Word of God and share Eucharist with the people of God. Over the last 53 years, those words have become more and more meaningful to me.

Since the Second Vatican Council, the following instruction is found in the Roman Missal:

"On Sundays and Holy Days of Obligation, there is to be a Homily at every Mass that is celebrated with the people attending, and it may not be omitted without grave reason. On other days, it is recommended, especially on weekdays of Advent, Lent, and Easter Time, as well as on other festive days and occasions when the people come to church in greater numbers." (#66)

The daily homily has been a godsend during the last 53 years for me. It has become both the foundation of my spirituality and my prayer life.

Since January 2013, I have been sharing my Sunday homilies on YouTube; you can access them by typing "Larry Hehman" in the search field at YouTube.com.

Two years ago, JR came and said, "Larry, I really like your homilies, they are so powerful. Why don't you publish them?"

I replied, "Why don't you? I'll help you!"

A year went by and Whit said, "Father, I like your homilies. Why don't you publish them?"

And once again I said, "Why don't you? I'll help you!"

Was the Spirit speaking?

These two gentlemen and I got together, prayed, trusted in the Spirit, and this book is the result.

Let me suggest that you use this book as a source of prayer and encounter with the Lord; read the two or three scriptures first and think about them—let the Lord speak to you as you sit with the sacred scriptures. After you have allowed the scriptures to speak to you, read my homily and still yourself again, allowing the Holy Spirit to enter your heart, imagination, mind, and soul. Then, truly, you are in the presence of the Lord. Then you are praying! Let God's Word, my thoughts, and your thoughts—together—become prayer deep within you.

Each of us listens to the Word of God and, because God's Word is living, we each hear it and experience it in our own way; the scriptures come alive for us because of our own unique circumstances and frame of reference. I, too, preach in my own way, like Rahner said, "fumbling, miserable, and often repetitious words—the holy, blessed, and powerful Word of God, the Word that brings God Himself and His eternal life into our midst." You might say I do it with a twist that is uniquely my own. Hence, the title of the book: *The Word of God . . . with a Twist.*

I pray that you find your own twist with God's word by the power of the Holy Spirit stirring you at your depths as you walk with Jesus in the scriptures.

Finally, I must tell you that every cent received through the sale of this book, and every gift that is shared in excess of the cost of this book, will be given to the Catholic Action Center, which serves our sisters and brothers in need in Lexington, Kentucky. If you ask me, the ministry of the Catholic Action Center is, for sure, the best homily!

—Fr. Larry Hehman

The
WORD
of
GOD
. . . with a
TWIST

180 GALLONS OF THE BEST WINE

Is 62:1–5
1 Cor 12:4–11
Jn 2:1–11

Our Gospel today deals with a great wedding reception in Cana, in Galilee. I've been a priest now for more than 50 years, and I have probably prepared and officiated at over 800 weddings. Every one of the couples that I married were prepared. I cannot recall any couple who was looking for their marriage to be a time of torment, unhappiness, and eventual divorce. A very good, positive, live-happily-ever-after attitude was prevalent.

For me, it's no wonder why in the Bible, God's love for us is presented as marital love.

Whether in the Song of Songs or the New Testament, Jesus is the groom and the church is the bride. Even in the Old Testament—the negative, the adulterous generation—when it comes to marriage, it's all positive and good; all is filled with expectation.

As I look at this Gospel, I see three insights: One has to do with Jesus's mother, so Mother Mary gives an insight. A good party gives an insight, and best of all, Jesus himself, gives an insight.

The first insight is Mary's. Mary, his mother; she loved these people. She and Jesus are there. She has compassion. She feels bad when they are running out of wine. With her compassion, she turns to Jesus and says, "Do something, Jesus."

This reminds me of a few weeks ago in the temple, when Jesus took off on his own and he was lost. Mary was very upset with Jesus and said, "Why have you done this to me and to your father?"

He told her, "Didn't you know that I must be about my father's business?"

At Canna, we hear a statement similar to that, when she says, "Do something for these people." He says, "It's not yet my time. It's none of my business. It's their problem. Their parents, their friends, their party."

Mary says, "Do whatever He tells you." Jesus tells the hosts of the party to bring the water jugs and wild things happen: 180 gallons of wine!

The second insight is an insight into a good party. You need good people; plenty of people; fun-loving, alive people; good food and plenty to drink. Whether it's wine or liquor or beer or soft drinks. That makes a good party, at least it is and has been my experience during my growing-up years in the Hehman family. Have plenty; don't run out.

The third insight is with Jesus and I think it is the best. He does not negate his mother. He does something because his mother asked. He didn't just say, "Too bad, so sad. Not my problem, it's theirs." No, he makes 180 gallons of wine and not just good wine, but "the best wine." As John's Gospel states, "Everyone serves the good wine first."

Then, when the people have drunk freely, the inferior wine. That's the norm. It's not the norm for Jesus. It's not the norm for God.

God does not create us just good. God creates us very good, as it says in the book of Genesis. Jesus not only loves us, He forgives us. God is not interested in our being tormented, like in a bad marriage, and He doesn't want us to make one another unhappy, like in a bad marriage. Or for us to eventually say, "The heck with it," and get a divorce. No, God is just the opposite of that.

God wants to do a good party. He calls it "the Kingdom of God." Jesus wants us to go to a good place: heaven. Jesus talks about good life: eternal life. "I've come to bring life and life in abundance." That's God talk or God's way or God's intention. It's like 180 gallons of good wine at a good party when we will all be with one another and be fulfilled. John says, "That's what this man, Jesus, is all about." That's what John says in the very beginning of his Gospel, in chapter 2. He says, "Jesus did this as the beginning of his signs and his disciples began to follow him."

You and I are his disciples, too. You and I follow him with the compassion and the love and the concern of his mother, with looking for the big party, the Kingdom of God, and we're looking forward to being with one another in eternal life.

If I want to do what Jesus tells me, what would I do differently? What would I do the same?

IT IS JUST THE GARDENER! BUT IS IT?

Acts 5:27–32
Rev 5:11–14
Jn 21:1–19

We often walk without realizing that Jesus is walking with us. Some people say Jesus walks in our shoes. At times dejected or joyful, up or down. These two people are much like us. They're walking seven miles together to the little village of Emmaus dejected because Jesus has been crucified.

I think we need to know a little bit about Emmaus. Go back 166 years before Christ. In the first book of Maccabees, chapter three, a general named Judah Maccabee had a great victory over another man with a strange-sounding name, Antiochus Epiphanes. Judah's army marched out and camped around Emmaus. They fought to restore the temple so that the Jewish people could pray and come together. The restoration of the temple that eventually came about is a great feast day in today's world and is called Hanukkah. It is celebrated around our holiday of Christmas, our feast of lights. Judah banked on God to help him. As it says in chapter four, "Let us cry out to heaven to see whether God will favor us and remember his covenant with our ancestors and crush this army. Then all the Gentiles will know that there is one who redeems and saves Israel." So, what happened? They were redeemed.

Well, more than a century and a half later, these two Jews, these two disciples, Cleophas and the other, walked seven miles from Jerusalem to this little village. They didn't have a victorious feeling; they had the agony of defeat. They had hoped that Jesus was going to be the Messiah, the redeemer and savior. Yet, what they had experienced was His crucifixion and death, and they were defeated. They were walking downcast. They didn't know that Jesus was alive, resurrected and walking beside them. They didn't recognize Him.

It is here, which is so important, where the Church changes to a new way of recognizing Jesus. It is here where Jesus makes Himself known to not just a few, but to many of us, revealing who He is, how He works now, how He appears now, and how He is present now. It happened when they stopped and invited Him in for supper. As it says, He took bread, blessed, and broke it. They recognized Him in the breaking of the bread. And then He disappeared.

When they reflected on this, the people in this small group said, "Were not our hearts burning within us while Jesus spoke to us on the way, when He opened the scriptures to us? Did we not know that something really deep and meaningful was taking place? Were we not encountering Jesus on the way?" And when He broke the bread and blessed it, they realized, "It is Jesus. He's not dead. He is alive. He is making himself known to us in a new way. We don't understand it, but He did, and He is gone. He vanished."

You and I are like those two disciples. We listen to the scriptures and hear Jesus. He is present where two or three are gathered. He is present in the Eucharist. We recognize Him in the breaking, the blessing, the giving of bread. It's no different. From that time on, that is how we recognize Christ.

Mary didn't recognize Him in the garden. She thought He was the gardener. She recognized Him in His word according to other accounts. Do you recognize Christ in His words, in His actions? I hope you do because that's the way it's going to be until the Second Coming. I think we should take advantage of the new way of recognizing and being with Jesus. We have no great disadvantage over those two disciples. They are like us.

Can I recognize Jesus in those who walk with me? Can I recognize Jesus in the migrant, the refugee, the LGBTQ sister or brother, the people on the peripheries?

Pride—The Good Kind

Am 8:4–7
1 Tim 2:2–8
Lk 16:1–13

Friday morning, I received a call from my agent at Merrill-Lynch, and he said, "You have a bond coming due, many thousands of dollars. Would you like to invest for another 5 percent?"

I said, "Sure, yes, go ahead."

And then I started to read the readings for this weekend—in particular, the very end of the Gospel where it says, "You cannot serve both God and Mammon." Another translation is: "You can't serve God and riches or money, and you can't make riches or money a false God." I paused to think about that.

But, also on Friday morning, I was very pleased in reading on the front page of the newspaper an article about Pope Francis. The headline read: "Pope offers striking new vision for the church." I really like that! I found that to be totally refreshing. I've a priest for 48 years now, and I look back on my life and think, Yes, I was from a very good Roman Catholic Christian community in Northern Kentucky. I went to four different seminaries, and I spent the last four years in a seminary in Austria, and I really had a Vatican II concept of the church as it unfolded from 1961 to 1965. I lived in Innsbruck with great theologians, and I sort of feel like I've become a Vatican II priest. Since my retirement, I get rather depressed sometimes; I feel as though the church is regressing to a pre-Vatican II church. And I was so excited about a Vatican II and post-Vatican church!

With Pope Francis, I'm excited again about our church and where it's headed. Rethinking is always a good thing—rethinking religion and thinking about what exactly Roman Catholicism is. What is church? What is religion? I looked up the definition of religion this morning in the dictionary and it says: "Religion, a belief in and reverence for, a supernatural power or powers." That is good, very generic. Very good, I think. When I took a class at the University of Kentucky on world religions, their bottom line or beginning line was this: religion is men's and women's response to God or ultimate forces. I've always liked that, because when I asked myself what true religion is, I found it's a true response and a valid response to God. Over all the millennia, our concept of religion has changed drastically, and, as I said—for me and the Church, especially—in the last 50 years, I think our concept of religion and Catholicism has changed drastically. I know, and I hope you do, too, that we must continue to change in understanding what is truth, what is religion, and what Jesus is calling us to do.

I find the pope so refreshing because I think he's taking us closer to what the vibrant Vatican II church was to be. I read in the local paper, the *Lexington Herald-Leader*, that the pope said, "The church had grown obsessed with abortion, gay marriage, and contraception." It seems that the only things we talked about for too long were abortion, gay marriage, and contraception. A few years back, I remember a priest who spoke about abortion at Christmas Mass. I'm not sure that approach will influence people!

The pope also said that the church has put dogma before love. You might hear statements that he makes where he puts love before dogma. He also said, at least in this article, that the church has prioritized moral doctrines over serving the poor and marginalized.

Wow! Isn't that great that he called attention to that? I'm excited with this pope. I think he's teaching—or more so, showing—true religion. I think he reflects and shows the basic message of Jesus Christ. I think he is leading us in the direction of vibrant Roman Catholicism. That's why I'm so proud of him, and that's why I'm maybe regaining a little of my former "I'm so happy and proud to be a Roman Catholic priest."

Are you proud of being a Roman Catholic? Are you proud of following Jesus Christ? What do you think? You cannot serve both God and money or Mammon. Whom do you serve? What is your response to divinity or the supernatural powers? It certainly is changing, and for some, it is rather exciting.

LOST AND FOUND—TOO GOOD TO BE TRUE?

Ex 32:7–11
1 Tim 1:12–17
Lk 15:1–32

There are three little parables or stories in the Gospel: one has to do with 100 sheep and losing one; another has to do with 10 coins and losing one; and the last is about a father having two sons and losing one.

Well, what would you like to talk about? The 100 sheep, losing one and finding one? How about the 10 coins? I have here four silver dollars. Some man in the parish used to give me a silver dollar every year, and he gave me about 10 of them. When I was getting ready to get all these silver dollars together, I lost one, but then I found it again. That's sort of like the 10 coins the woman had, or maybe you like the prodigal son story—the two sons, and the father.

The pope has repeatedly asked us to be people of mercy. A few years ago, he even declared a Year of Mercy. He really wants us to be like God—merciful and loving understanding and forgiving.

Let's look at the parable. This is really about a happy father. It's about a renegade son and a bitter son, but I like to focus on—not the prodigal son or the bitter older son—but on the happy father.

I don't understand why they call this the prodigal son story. Why not the angry brother story or why not the happy father story? The father, to me, is what it is all about. This father in the parable is like God is for us. This father was so compassionate and understanding with his sons. He ran out to the prodigal son; he didn't even wait for him to get home! He ran out to meet him, he embraced him, he kissed him, he gave him the finest robe, he put a ring on his finger, and he put sandals or shoes on his feet. He threw a great big party. I love parties! He threw a great big party for this renegade son of his. He took the best calf and had it cooked, and he celebrated. He screams out, "He was dead. He's not dead. He's alive again; he's back."

This parable, I think, is the way God is with us, whether we're like son number one, dirty son-of-a-gun renegade, or we're like son number two, goody-two-shoes who always does the right thing. But don't forget at the very end of that story, that son was about to leave. "You never threw a party for me, and you do all this for him!" That loving father had problems with both sons, not just one son.

You and I are like either son, or maybe a combination of both of them. But are we as good as that loving, happy father? We don't even know the rest of the story, and we shouldn't—it's a parable, the story is open-ended. We'll never know the rest of the story of those two sons: how they lived or if they lived. This is a parable to teach us something: to teach us about how God acts towards all of us, whether we're son number one, or son number two, or a son-of-a-gun number three.

It's almost too good to be true. God is so good and so perfect, loving, compassionate, just, and merciful. You find some coins or that one that's really important and then say, "Oh, I found it," or you might find your daughter or your son, a human, and love them and forgive them, and rejoice.

That's the way God is for you and for me, it's almost, almost too good to be true.

Which of those three parables do you like? Why does it speak to you?

THE UNJUST JUDGE

Ex 17:8–13
2 Tm 3:14–4:2
Lk 18:1–8

Both of these readings of scripture deal with prayer: your prayer, and my prayer.

In the Gospel, a woman, a widow, goes to the unjust judge, and she continues to bother him and press him for a just decision, and he doesn't give one. I mean, he's an unjust judge. She pesters him so much that he finally gives up and says, "I don't fear God or anybody else, but in this world, I can't take this woman, this widow. She's wearing me out." For the sake of her persistence, he renders a just decision. Her request, which was very important, was answered.

We're supposed to pray like that widow, persistently. We're supposed to wear God out, so to speak: pray constantly. No matter what you say, or what you ask for, or how you pray. The thing is, raise your mind and heart to God always.

The Old Testament reading I like even more because this is when I began, on a regular basis, to do some Hehman Hokey Homily Helpers. It was on this particular Sunday, with these particular two readings.

Moses says, "Look, Aaron, I'm going to go up to the top of the hill or we are, and I'm going to pray to the Lord for our success."

So, he does. He prays with his hands up to the heavens and he prays for their success. As long as he prayed and looked to the heavens with his hands up, the Jews were winning the battle. But he got tired.

So, here is my Hehman Hokey Homily Helper: I went to my library and I got eight volumes of the *Catholic Encyclopedia.* That was 20 years ago when I could hold eight for a while, and I said, "I'm going to give you this homily and I'm going to stand here and give this homily only as long as I can hold these eight volumes." And so I began my homily and I was in a bit of a hurry to finish . . . the way, very often in our prayer life, we're in a hurry to finish.

When we get tired of praying, we need to keep praying. When we don't feel like praying, we need to keep praying.

We help one another pray when we pray in community, together. That's called public prayer. That's the public worship and prayer of the community. You and I, we do it together. That is probably the best—might not feel the best, but it might be the best because we do it alongside Jesus and offer up Jesus too, so, we pray with Jesus and receive Jesus in the Eucharist. But certainly, when we pray privately, that's good, too.

When we pray privately, we're more often like a child—a child of God. You know what a child asks for? Anything, everything, and the ridiculous. When I was a kid, my next-door neighbor was Oscar Rummel III, when we were in the third or fourth grade. He would go to his dad all the time and he said, "Dad, for my birthday, will you get me a pony?" He kept on going, "Dad will you get me . . ."

"Okay, Oscar, I'll get you a pony on your birthday, but it's going to be your eighth or your 10th or something."

Oscar kept on asking his dad for a pony. You know what? We lived in the city!

A little kid will ask for anything. Sometimes, our prayer life is like asking for a pony in the middle of the city. Parents don't care. You're a parent; you don't care what your kid asks for. You may get bugged: "Quiet. Later. Promise. Later."

Jesus tells his people, "Pray like a child. Pray like that widow. Pray like Moses. Pray up a storm and don't give up. You will never, ever be disappointed. You might not get your will, but you won't be disappointed. Your prayer will be effective."

Our prayer will be effective if we pray properly—you have to add: "Not my will, but Thy will be done." Ask anything. Be persistent. Get help. Pray together. Thy will be done.

How can I make my prayer more effective? Do I believe God will be a just judge in my regard or do I try to manipulate God?

WHAT'S NEW?

Acts 14:21–27
Rv 21:1–5
Jn 13:31–35

What's new?

In the Gospel, Jesus said, "I give you a new commandment, love one another." I don't think that's so new. In fact, if you look it up, Jesus is quoting the book of Leviticus 19:18: "You shall love your neighbor as yourself. I'm the Lord."

So, what's new about that? Jesus keeps quoting the Old Testament. On another passage, Jesus says in Mark 12:30, "You shall love the Lord your God with your heart, with all your soul, with all your mind, and all your strength." What's new about that? I think nothing. Jesus once again is quoting the Old Testament. He quotes Deuteronomy 6:4-6: "Hear O Israel, the Lord is our God. The Lord alone. Therefore, you shall love the Lord your God will all your heart, all your soul, and all your strength."

Jesus is quoting the books of Leviticus and Deuteronomy, and he says these things so well. I always think Jesus really wanted to be a good Jew. He saw a lot of things wrong in the Jewish tradition in his time, and he would go back to the Old Testament many years back and he would say, "That's not what God really said. Yahweh said this," and he quotes it. And it comes out almost as if it is new.

I think it was only in due time that Jesus began to realize that he was really something special, that he was the son of God, that he was the Messiah and that he and the Father were one. When Jesus said, "Love one another," that was new, in a sense, because this awareness that all and everything in the world and in the universe is terribly and totally connected. Even in the cosmos, everything is connected. Everything is connected in the cosmos, in the world, and on planet earth.

We are connected with each other and with God, but sometimes we don't realize it. Whenever we love one, we love all. When we hate one, we hate all. Jesus said, "So, whatsoever you do to the least of my brothers and sisters, you do to me." That is, whatever we do, we do to Jesus, to God, to the church, to the Kingdom of God. Do we really realize how connected we really are?

Here is something I read this week: "We must help people connect to the story, the mystery of God and the mystery of the universe, so that we can all understand the significance of our lives as part of the body of Christ and the great pattern in things which Jesus calls the Kingdom of God." More than ever before, we must discover a common meaning, a shared story to give our lives a purpose and harmony. Perhaps cosmology and science itself can help to bring us together toward a common goal of saving our planet and saving ourselves. What happens in the Middle East is important. What happens in the hills of Kentucky is important. What happens in my family is important.

How can I live more intentionally as a person connected to others in my community, parish, world?

FOLLOW ME

1 Kgs 19:26, 29–21
Gal 5:1, 13–18
Lk 9:51–62

These readings focus on the calling of our Lord Jesus to biblical characters and to us, to follow. We are all called to be disciples of Christ.

In First Kings, Elijah, the prophet, following the order given him by God, seeks out Elisha as the prophet to succeed him. Elisha says yes. He makes a commitment to give his whole life to prophesy—a total and great commitment.

In the passage from Luke, Jesus is traveling to Jerusalem and encountering on the way men who want to be his followers. To the first man, Jesus gives a warning that it is a difficult life that he is choosing. That this man has no idea what Jesus is asking for.

To a second man, who asks to be permitted to return home and bury his father, Jesus says, "Let the dead bury the dead," and tells him he must totally give himself to following Jesus right now. To a third man, who wants to go and say good-bye to family, Jesus again insists, "No one who sets a hand to the plow and looks to what was left behind is fit for the Kingdom of God." Jesus wants an immediate response of, "I'll do it right now."

As we are all called to follow Jesus, we realize that it is not an easy decision to make. In our youth, we are struggling just to make decisions about our careers. In our middle age, we find ourselves wondering if we truly are following Jesus in our lives. Even in our twilight years, we wonder if we have lived our lives as true followers of Jesus. We ask ourselves, "Did I really follow the Lord?"

In a prayer by Thomas Merton, I find peace of mind. In his prayer, he acknowledges that he has no idea where he is going, cannot see the road ahead of him, that if he thinks he is following God's will, that is not necessarily true. Merton concludes that the fact that he has the desire to please God pleases God. He prays that he will never do anything apart from that desire.

When we ask ourselves if we are followers of Christ, we can be certain that if we are free from prejudice, and respect and love our neighbors as much as we love ourselves, we are sincerely trying to be followers.

A Prayer of
Thomas Merton

My Lord God, I have no idea where I am going. I do not see the road ahead of me. Nor do I really know myself, and the fact that I think I am following your will does not mean that I am actually doing so.

But I believe that the desire to please you does in fact please you. And I hope that I will never do anything apart from that desire. And I know that if I do this, you will lead me by the right road. Though I may know nothing about it.

Therefore, will I trust you always, though I may seem to be lost and in the shadow of death I will not fear, for you are ever with me, and you will never leave me to face my struggles alone. Amen.

THE BODY AND
BLOOD OF CHRIST

Gn 14:18–20
I Cor 11:23–26
Lk 9: 11–17

Feast of Corpus Christi (Most Holy Body and Blood of Christ)

I like the proverb, "Eat, drink, and be merry, for tomorrow, you die."
At least the first part of that: eat, drink, and be merry.

We're all prone to do this. We want to eat, drink, and be merry.
That steak, that lobster or whatever; that favorite libation, whether
it be a Coca Cola or a beer; and that luscious fruit or sweet candy.
Eat, drink, and be merry. Take it all in, and we want to take it all in
during life. All that we can eat. You can even take it all in sexually in
life. Take it all in; look out to the world and take it all in.

We want to see the world. That's the way we are; that's the drive that
we have. Take it all in, and geographically eat, drink and be merry.

This is even real regarding God. God is all good. God is beautiful,
powerful, just, merciful. Take it all in. That same thing applies to
Jesus. Jesus is God; take Jesus in.

If Jesus is in that little wafer, that bread, or in that cup of wine, take
it all in. It does require that you believe. If you really believe in God,
and that God is present, take him all in. It's even better than that

juicy steak. It's even better than sex. It's even better than a trip to California or to the moon or to Mars, or anywhere in the universe!

Take God in. We celebrate the Feast of the Most Holy Body and Blood of Jesus Christ. Take in the body and blood of Jesus Christ. Now it is, without a doubt, a mystery, how it all happens, but the key in understanding this mystery is the principle that the greater absorbs the lesser. In other words, when you eat the apple or the steak, the apple or steak becomes part of you.

When you take Jesus in, his body and blood, in reality, Jesus doesn't become part of you, but you become part of the greater reality, you become part of Jesus, of God. That's an amazing principle. You know, taking it all in, Jesus Christ, body, and blood is even much greater and more important than sitting in front of the blessed sacrament for an hour.

Receiving communion, you take in Jesus Christ, and you become an intimate part of the body of Christ. Really? Yes, really! Do we totally understand that? No, but we do it because Jesus said, "Here, I give you my body and my blood. Eat it, drink it. Do this in remembrance of me." Yes. When we do that, we become a greater part of the body of Christ.

You have taken him in, but in reality, God has taken you in. You become more holy and pleasing to God. Oh yes, it requires faith and belief. The deeper your faith, the more you appreciate this reality. It's true, especially true when you're conscious of it, when you have faith. Even if you do not have faith, though, it's still true: this is the real presence of the body and blood of Jesus Christ. Do you believe that? I do. It's been my life, celebrating the Eucharist. Preaching and the Eucharist are the most two important things in my life and what I enjoy the most.

So, I like that proverb, "Eat, drink, and be merry." I don't like that latter part too much, where tomorrow you die. But before you die, take it all in. You'll be happier, you'll be better. Believe it or not, you will even be holier. Holy and pleasing to God.

The miracle that Jesus performed with those five loaves and two fish for the crowd of five thousand still continues when He feeds us His body and blood in the Eucharist. Spend some time with this miracle and try to appreciate the unfathomable gift that is ours.

BADGERING GOD
AND DAD, TOO!

Gn 18:20–32
Col 2:12–14
Lk 11:1–13

Today let's deal with ordinary things, like how we pray and how often we ask for things in prayer—persistence in prayer.

Remember when we were kids, we would play one parent against another? Mom against dad, and dad against mom. You got an answer that you didn't like from your mom, so you went to your dad and vice versa. You played them, one against the other, until you finally got one of them to say okay.

One thing I remember vividly is during the heat of July, we always wanted to go swimming. We liked to go to this playground called Ross. It's in Ross, Kentucky (a little place about 10 miles outside of Northern Kentucky). They had two pools there filled with artesian well water. When they would fill those pools, side by side, they would be very cold. The initial plunge was torture, it'd take days for the water to warm up. We would bug our parents over and over, "Let's go swimming. Come on Dad; let's go. Let's call Uncle Norb."

They had five kids and we had five kids in our family. Finally, my dad would say, "Okay, go call your uncle or your cousins and see if they want to go swimming at Ross," and we would. On a Saturday or a Sunday afternoon, we would go there, prepare hamburgers, corn

31

on the cob, and baked beans, and we would swim all afternoon. Both families played together at the swimming pool because of our persistence with our parents. Often, our cousins bugged their parents, too.

In the readings this morning, Abraham is rather persistent with God. "You know that Sodom and Gomorrah that you're going to rain down terror on? Hey, there are innocent people there. Are you going to kill the innocent people along with the guilty? What if there are 50 innocent people?"

"Ah, 50? I won't," God says.

Abraham baits the hook. "What if there's 45, 40?"

"Still won't."

"What if there's 30, 20? Or what if there's only 10 innocent people in Sodom? Are you going to kill them with all the guilty?"

And through the persistence and prayer of Abraham asking God to do this, God finally says, in the book of Genesis, "For the sake of the 10, I will not destroy it."

Pretty good, pretty good. Often that's the way we pray. Just like with our parents: "Can we," "May we . . ." and they say, "Okay, let's do it." Persistence!

Well, in this same way, I think the disciples asked Jesus, "Teach us to pray," and he gives them the perfect prayer: Our Father.

And then Jesus tells the disciples what God is not like. God is not like a bad parent who's cruel, violent, negative, and threatening. Jesus uses an example of what God is not like: God is not like a father when you say, "Please, Dad, can I have a fish sandwich or a big Mac?" and He gives you a sandwich, but it's a snake sandwich! That's not what God is like. Or, God is not like a bad parent when you say, "I want a fried egg for breakfast," and your mom or your dad fries you up not an egg, but a scorpion or a rat. Parents aren't like that. They love their children and they try to give them, within reason, what is good for their children.

You know what? All that Abraham did, badgering and asking and bugging God—"Don't destroy the town and the innocent people"—I think Jesus likes that. Might not be the highest form of prayer, but Jesus still likes it because we're raising our mind and heart to God who loves us.

I think I have come to believe that God is like my dad. It's pretty powerful to say something about your dad that way, but God is a great parent, and infinitely much more. How do you pray?

Do I badger God or am I persistent in prayer? Do I believe God is really a good parent who will do the best for me?

HOSPITALITY

Gn 18:1–10
Col 1:24–28
Lk 10:38–42

I'd like to discuss hospitality. What I find the most interesting is where the Gospel talks about Martha and Mary and their hospitality towards Jesus. I think we all love this because, in a sense, we're all Martha or Mary or both.

Jesus says to Martha, "Martha, Martha, you are anxious and worried about many things. There is need of only one thing. Mary has chosen the better part, and it will not be taken from her."

"Only one thing," Jesus says. What is that one thing? What is Jesus talking about? I confess, I really don't know what this one thing is!

I racked my brain and I thought—and I ask you to rack your brain, too. What is this one thing?

Maybe Mary, as opposed to Martha, is with Jesus and she's looking for meaning in life, and she's experiencing the goodness of Jesus?

Or, maybe Mary is trying to figure out her true self while Martha is out there rattling all the pots and pans in the kitchen, trying to whip up a meal, getting upset?

Or, maybe Mary is really happy with Jesus. She's seeking God or she's seeking Jesus. Or, maybe it's just Mary's seeking God. We know Jesus is God, and she's attracted to that. Is that the one thing?

Well, all of these are halfway decent attempts to figure out what that one thing is, but in reality, I don't absolutely know what that one thing is. You just have to rack your own heart and your brain.

Are you a person like Martha worrying about getting everything together, worrying about everything here and now, worrying about what's going on? Or are you a person more like Mary, who's more interested in that one thing—a relationship or meaning or goodness, trying to find God?

How hospitable am I, or are we? Is your parish hospitable? Is it known for making people feel welcome? Do you greet people when they come to your parish; do you talk to them? Do you help them and find out their needs and invite them to become part of the parish?

I looked at my parish bulletin and I am happy there is still a note of hospitality on the front page. It says we welcome to our worship all who are embraced by Jesus's love. Saints and sinners, people of every race, language, and color. The immigrant, refugee, and alien. The poor and the affluent, those born with sexual ambiguity or differing orientation. The divorced, separated, the hurting, and the alienated. Those who are inquiring into the faith and inactive Catholics. We embrace you with the love of Jesus.

Is your parish hospitable? Your business? Your home? Your city? Your country, especially regarding immigrants? While you are here on earth, practice hospitality. Remember Jesus said, "Whatsoever you do to the least of my brothers and sisters, you do to me." Hospitality is a real Christian virtue.

Lord, help me become more hospitable and to think of the comfort and well-being of others over my own.

What Must I Do to Get into Heaven?

Dt 30:10–14
Col 1:15–20
Lk 10:25–37

A young scholar poses a very good question to Jesus. It is a question for which we all seek an answer. The question is, "What must I do to enter into eternal life?"

Jesus, giving an answer to the scholar, reaches back a thousand years to the Old Testament books of Leviticus and Deuteronomy. In Leviticus, we are told to love our neighbor as we love ourselves, and in Deuteronomy, we are instructed to love God with our whole heart, being, strength, and mind.

Those answers were true in Old Testament times, in Jesus's time, and now in our modern world. The answer is the same.

Jesus goes further, giving an example for everyone to follow. In the example, we have a person who is in need. He has been robbed, beaten, and left helpless alongside the road. A priest and a Levite, setting a bad example, walk by him without acknowledging that he is even there.

Then, along comes a "foreigner," a man who is a Samaritan. He is moved by compassion for the suffering and defenseless man. He takes him to safety and provides for his needs. Jesus asks, "Who is his neighbor?"

This parable serves to educate us now, as it did throughout scriptural time. In today's world, there is much suffering. Do we notice it? Do we feel and show compassion?

Getting into heaven, according to Jesus, is very connected with how we answer those questions. And as it says in Deuteronomy, finding and loving God is not all that mysterious or difficult. He is not in the sky, across the sea. He is here with us and very near to us. He is in our mouths and in our hearts.

How do we get into heaven? It is by being compassionate, loving our neighbor and our God. It is by connecting with the "others" in the world who need our help and caring. Jesus is our model. His compassion toward us led him to his suffering and death on the cross.

Gracious God, help me never walk past or ignore the suffering of others, but to the best of my ability, help me reach out and show compassion as Jesus does.

AM I A DISCIPLE OF JESUS?

Is 66:10–14
Gal 6:14–18
Lk 10:1–12, 17–20

I am going to translate six words from the Gospel. I am not translating from one language to another. I am translating the words as said in the Gospel to their meaning in today's modern world. Just as Jesus sought disciples in his time, he is calling us to become his disciples today.

The first word from the Gospel that I am translating is "harvest." The harvest then, and now, refers to people, all the people in existence. The act of harvesting refers to the work of bringing them into the Kingdom of God.

Next, we have the word "abundant." The harvest is abundant. There are billions of people in the world today. The harvest is to include all people of all times: past, present, and future.

The harvest requires "laborers." This is the next word I am translating. Laborers, disciples of Jesus who will teach and preach the Good News, are needed. The work, as Jesus explains, is not easy. We face the same problems as did the disciples of old. We may not be accepted by those to whom we reach out. We must care about how we are to shelter and feed ourselves.

Laborers for Jesus are the laity. They are baptized Christians/ Catholics. They are the clergy, a group that is shrinking in numbers in this current time. The Church is called to confront this very complex problem. Prayer for more young men to join the priesthood is not enough. It is a simplistic attempt, not able to address the complexity of the problem.

In laboring we must not dictate to or intimidate others. We must be Christ. Let other people see your joy and your goodness. You will win over many more Christians that way than if you are critical and blaming.

The last two words are the "lambs" and the "wolves." You and I, and all the baptized who know the message of Jesus are the lambs.

The world, people not receptive, who haven't accepted the message, the spirit, of Jesus, are the wolves.

These six words are words we need to better understand. If we do, we can be messengers, bearers of the message of Jesus Christ, and disciples helping to build the Kingdom of God.

Gracious God, help me be a good disciple of Jesus; help me work energetically to bring about the Kingdom of God in my corner of the world.

AM I RICH?

Eccl 1:2, 2:21–23
Col 3:1–5, 9–11
Lk 12:13–21

Are you rich? Would you like to be rich? I bet most people would say, "I'm not wealthy." How many people would like to be wealthy even if they're not? At any rate, what's wrong with wanting to be rich? I think my answer is: nothing. Nothing's wrong with being wealthy or rich, but there's always the "but." Catch what Jesus is saying. What He is saying to the crowd—and really, that crowd is us—is, "Guard against greed and one's life does not consist of possessions."

How would you like to run a college like Centre College in Danville, Kentucky, and out of the blue, this week comes $250 million to help you? Wouldn't that be nice? I'm sure you wouldn't complain about $250 million. I'd like to win the lottery. That's another $250 million for somebody if I won it! Would you like to win the lottery? Would you like to be wealthy?

Jesus asks us to look at ourselves relative to wealth, riches, and possessions. You know, I feel like I'm a rich priest, not that I have that much money, but for a priest, I think I have enough money. In all honesty, I sort of think or feel that I need money. I grew up in a large family and my father had two jobs, and we had a lot of sickness in the family. My father owed more than he had; however, we really had a good family life, even if we didn't have much money.

When I was a kid, we didn't have enough money even to pay for the medical bills for my mother, who was dying of cancer; I think it sort of got to me. I feel that I need something on the side or on the shelf, or in the bank to give me some security. I'm not bragging about that. I think it is insecurity more than security! Nothing's wrong with wanting security or wanting to have some money in the bank for when you are going to need it.

The bottom line, I think, is that Jesus is trying to tell the crowd and us: keep on asking yourself about your need for possessions or money. What do you really *need* versus what do you *want*? What are your possessions in life? What are your values, what do you possess as values?

What about my "possession" of my faith or lack thereof? My health or lack thereof? What are my possessions? My possessions are multiple, material, spiritual, intellectual, social. I think it's good for us to ask, "Where am I with my possessions?" At the end of the Gospel, Jesus gives that clincher. Think about it, folks. When the person builds up all these things in barns, in bank accounts, in homes and drawers and storage units, Jesus says, "Look. This night, your life will be demanded of you and the things you have prepared, to whom will they belong? Thus would be for all those who store up treasures for themselves but are not rich in what matters to God."

What matters to God? What matters to me? What are my possessions? Where is my heart? Good questions. I ask myself often, and I ask you to ask yourself those same things, those same questions. What do I really have? What are my possessions? Which ones are important? Where am I? I hope you win the lottery!

> *Gracious God, you have given me so much. Really, I have already won the lottery. Thank you for everything. Yes, for everything!*

No Room in the Inn

Sir 3:2–6, 12–14
Col 3:12–21
Lk 2:41–52

Mary and Joseph had to travel to meet requirements that they register with the government, and they traveled with difficulty. Mary was pregnant with Jesus. For sure, that condition would make travel very difficult and uncomfortable. And then, when they arrived in Bethlehem, there was no room for them in the inn.

Jesus is the very antithesis of having no room. Jesus always has room for us at his inn. Jesus treats us the opposite way of how the world treated Jesus, Mary, and Joseph.

We are called to follow Jesus in his welcoming of all. As the world is dealing with large numbers of displaced people, homeless people, and those fleeing suffering in their home countries, we must welcome them and extend safety to them. Many countries are doing just that. I think they are acting like Jesus.

In the parable of the Good Samaritan, Jesus asks us to consider who our neighbors are. It is obvious to me that the parable is identifying everyone as our neighbor, including the foreigner, and as someone we need to invite into the inn.

In our world, we are constantly struggling with issues of equality. We seem to seek, but not be able to attain, equality of the races, acceptance of sexual orientation, the equality of women, and the list goes on. The basic message of this baby of Bethlehem is "love your neighbor as yourself." Love all and treat everyone as you would Jesus himself, and make room for everyone in your inn.

Finally, and most importantly, do we invite Christ into our inn? Do we welcome this Messiah, this Christ, this baby of Bethlehem, this God into the inn of our hearts? Do we take Him in and welcome Him?

Is this not the message of the first Christmas? The world may not have welcomed the Holy Family, the baby Jesus, into the inn, but Jesus has shown us how to welcome everybody else into that inn.

Gracious God, help me to never turn my back on those in need, but instead help me welcome, with all my heart, every sister and brother.

DOUBTING THOMAS AND THE 51ST ANNIVERSARY OF MY PRIESTHOOD

Acts 5:12–16
Rv 1:9–11, 12–13, 17–19
Jn 20:19–31

The bottom line in today's Gospel reading is that Jesus lives; he is alive now. That is the heart of our faith. This new Jesus, with a new resurrected body, is living today in the very best way. Jesus lives in me and he lives in you.

I have served as a priest for 51 years, and Jesus lives in me in many ways. He works in me, and I am happy and feel privileged that he uses me in priestly work. Jesus lives in me when I say the Eucharistic words: "This is my body, this is my blood." I am not saying these words; Jesus is. It is the new resurrected Jesus who says, "Here, take this and eat; take this and drink." He becomes present all over the world through the Eucharist.

While during a confession, I say the words "I forgive your sins," I don't have the power to forgive sins. Jesus has put me in that role. As we learn in today's Gospel, Jesus says to his disciples, "Receive the Holy Spirit, whose sins you forgive, they are forgiven." It is the power of Jesus, the spirit of Jesus, the Holy Spirit that forgives sins.

When I baptize, I say the words, "I baptize you in the name of the Father, Son, and Holy Spirit." This proves once more that Jesus is alive and present with us now. I also celebrate the sacrament of the sick. Jesus cured many people before his death and resurrection. He continues to speak words of healing through his priests.

Jesus is also alive in you. You speak for Jesus. Jesus was a great prophet; we are all called to be prophets. We are called to speak Jesus to the world. We are called to express the will, the mind, and the words of God to all humankind.

At times, we may find ourselves struggling with our faith. We may feel that our faith is not the richest, most intense, or the deepest. We may feel as if we are behaving as did Thomas when he doubted the Lord's divinity.

We must actively strive to increase our faith. We are called to be believers in Jesus and to trust in Jesus.

We each make an effort to establish the Kingdom of God. We believe in Jesus; we believe he is alive and resurrected. We believe that he is continuing to work in the world, in His Church, and in His kingdom until the end of time.

Gracious God, help me have a stronger faith in you. Help me bring Jesus to the world.

INRI

2 Sm 5:1–3
Col 1:12–20
Lk 23:35–43

In the Gospel reading for today, we find Jesus, still alive, but hanging on the cross. A sign with the letters INRI has been placed above his head by Pontius Pilate. These letters, though described differently in different languages, are translated to read, "This is Jesus, King of the Jews."

The scripture for today elaborates on what happened as Jesus was dying. Those present are mostly jeering at him and abusing him. The crowd is comprised of regular people, rulers, soldiers, and two thieves who are being crucified with Jesus.

The crowd is taunting Jesus: "If you are King of the Jews, then save yourself." The soldiers join in the taunts. The two thieves also have something to say to Jesus.

One thief, described as the bad thief, joins the taunting of the crowd. He says, "If you are the King of the Jews, save yourself and us, who are being crucified with you."

The second thief, however, recognizes the legitimacy of Jesus. He rebukes the other thief and points out, that while he and the other thief have been justly condemned, Jesus is innocent and has done nothing wrong. He asks Jesus to remember him when Jesus comes into his kingdom. Then Jesus says the beautiful words, "Today you will be with me in paradise."

This Jesus, hanging on the cross, this human person, this son of Mary and Joseph, this man from Nazareth, is much more than just a human person. He is the Chosen One, the Anointed One, the Christ, the Messiah. The Christ of God who is God. He, with God, is the creator of the universe. His existence has given the universe all dignity and new meaning. This Jesus, hanging on the cross, is indeed our Lord Jesus Christ, King of the Universe.

While we all might have some likeness to the people in the crowd, we have been touched by this man from Nazareth, who is indeed the son of God. Through his presence here he has touched and redeemed the universe.

So, Jesus came, and he served the whole cosmos, the whole universe. He did not do it as the kings throughout the history of mankind, as tyrants and dictators, but He did it as a suffering servant. He suffered and died for the salvation of the world.

His title, most truly, is "Jesus Christ, King of the Universe."

Gracious God, I am humbled and struck with awe by the beautiful love of Jesus. Help me follow him and love like he loved.

OPEN, READ, PREACH

Neh 8:2–4, 5–6, 8–10
1 Cor 12:12–30
Lk 1:1–4, 14–21

Let's look at Ezra in the first reading. He was a scribe and a priest around 450 BC. The Jews were returning from captivity in Babylon. They had been freed by Cyrus the Great, a Persian conqueror. The king said, "You're free. Go home, go back to Jerusalem." They did, but for 50 or 60 years before, they hadn't lived their religion and therefore were ignorant regarding their religion. Back in Jerusalem, Ezra preached Jewish law and Jewish scripture. They got so involved in it all, they rebuilt the temple some 500 years before Christ.

Now, about 450 years later, Jesus went to a very small synagogue in Nazareth where He grew up. There were only about 30 families in that little village. He was handed a scroll, which He opened. He read from it and preached from it. He said, "Look, the Spirit of the Lord is upon me," the first words in the scroll written by Isaiah.

Today, two thousand years later, I take a book, walk across the altar to the ambo and read out of the book, and preach on it: preaching on the Word of God, whether it is the Word of God in the Old Testament, or the Word of God coming out of Jesus's mouth, or Jesus's priesthood coming out of the mouth of the priest in the homily.

Homilies takes place at the ambo. In Jerusalem at the time of Ezra, they built a large, high place for him to stand, read, and speak so everybody in the crowd could see and hear. They had to listen, and he had to project his voice. That's exactly how it was done 2,500 years ago. Jesus, in His small synagogue in Nazareth, with a small number of families would do that: He would need to get up high and do the exact same thing: open, read, and preach.

We have a medium-sized church at Pax Christi. We need a microphone system and we need to be elevated a little bit, so we need an ambo. Look at the size of the altar in your church and see if it is larger and looks more important than the podium. Look at the altar in our cathedral, Christ the King, and compare it to the size of the podium. When we built Pax Christi, we thought the altar is important, but of equal importance is the Word of God. So, we built a podium that is sort of equal in size to the altar.

My point is this: Do you take the word of God seriously? Some people read the scriptures before they even come to church. I think that is wonderful! In fact, reading and preparing the homily has been the key to my prayer life for the last 47 years. I read, pray, and think about the readings before getting up to say something about them.

Do you take the Word of God seriously? I hope so. The Gospel is the word of Jesus. When Ezra went to the podium, the people stood up. We do the same thing when we read the Gospel. May the Word of God be in my mind and on my lips and in my heart. Really? Is it? If it is, I guarantee that you'll be a better person and that you will connect with God, and that you will be a happier person.

What does it mean for the Word of God to be on my lips? In my heart? Is the Word of God alive by the way I live my life?

A Leaf

Mal 3:19–20
2 Thes 3:7–12
Lk 21:5–19

Our scriptures today are elaborating on the coming of the "end of time." At this time of the year, as the fall season is ending, you surely must notice the presence of leaf machines visiting neighborhoods and sucking up all those leaves.

I like to look at the coming of the end of fall, and the coming of the end of time, as being similar, as they both involve falling leaves. You and I are like leaves.

We are like leaves because we come and go. Just as leaves begin in the spring and are filled with juices and sap and help produce fruit and flowers, we, in our early lives, are capable of regenerating and producing much fruit.

In the fall, just as the leaves dry out and eventually drop off the tree, go into the ground, or into the leaf-mulching machine, we too are like the leaves in that we reach a time in life where we become dried out and ready to go into the ground.

Everything comes to an end. Jesus, in today's Gospel, looking at a beautifully adorned temple, explains that even that temple will come to its end. One stone will not be upon another. Whether you are a temple, a leaf, or a human being, we all come to our end in this present life.

Jesus, in another part of scripture, looks at the city of Jerusalem and weeps because he sees that Jerusalem and its people will come to an end. He, through his earthly life, becomes more and more aware that he will suffer and die.

It is in the nature of things that this will happen. It is going to happen to you, it is going to happen to me, and even to Creation itself. We, however, are promised a life after death. In a preface for funerals, we are told that life has not ended, it has changed. Our leaf will fall off the tree, but our leaf will be changed. It will not go out of existence and be mulched up in the leaf machine. We will be carried over to the resurrection of the body. We will go back to the God who created us.

This is our hope. It happened to Jesus. He was resurrected. Mary was taken into heaven. It is going to happen to you and me.

We will not go into a mulching machine. We will go into a new phase of existence. We will have life in a new resurrected body.

Gracious God, thank you for loving me and choosing to keep me with you through all eternity.

Odor of Sanctity

Zep 3:14–18
Phil 4:4–7
Lk 3:10–18

The Gospel reading for today is all about John the Baptist. He was such a powerful and oddly attractive man. He was very positive in his outlook and preaching and was spreading the Good News. Many people left the city of Jerusalem and went to him in the desert. These people were seeking holiness, goodness, and happiness and were drawn to John the Baptist, hoping to find it.

This attraction to John the Baptist calls to mind a phrase I have heard, the "Odor of Sanctity." This phrase indicates that holiness, with all of its wonderful and positive characteristics, also emits a very pleasant scent.

At one time, this phrase was used to describe individuals who had the stigmata. They had such a sweet smell. You might have thought they would have had a very unpleasant smell due to their wounds and the fact that their flesh might have been rotting.

Another example of sanctity having such a sweet odor is from the life of Saint Theresa, the Little Flower of Lisieux. The Odor of Sanctity was all around her. When she died, at an early age, the entire convent where she lived and died smelled of roses, the Odor of Sanctity.

As a child my religious experience included roses being given to us after novenas and prayers. I remember a song to St. Theresa asking her "not to turn away, but to drop down one little rose."

So, when the crowds went to find John the Baptist in the desert, they were seeking help so that they might obtain holiness. The crowds asked him what they must do to become holy. He told them to share: share your food, clothing, money, time, yourselves. Share love, the virtue of love.

When tax collectors asked how they may become holy, he told them to exemplify justice in their work, not to cheat and "cook the books."

When soldiers came seeking help, he told them they must not misuse or abuse their power and authority. Use your authority equally for the rich and the poor and for the black and the white.

The message of John the Baptist and Jesus Christ is all positive. Both men spoke about joy and positive Good News.

As we celebrate this third week of Advent, I hope your religious experience is that of following Jesus into joy and goodness, leading you to be happier and better people.

Gracious God, help me to look beyond my disappointments and see the possibilities that are offered by the positive and powerful messages given by John the Baptist and Jesus. Help me believe.

MODERN LEPROSY IN NEED OF A CURE

2 Kgs 5:14–17
2 Tm 2:8–13
Lk 17:11–19

Two of today's readings deal with society's treatment of people with leprosy, also called Hansen's disease. What does the disease really represent and is there anything like that in today's society?

The lepers were those who were out of order or unclean. In society, they were pushed off to the side, pushed out of society because they were unclean. The leper was not considered a sinner but unclean and therefore a leper couldn't be around others. The leper was not allowed to go to the temple and worship because of his or her disease. A leper was not allowed to even live in the city or the village because of the disease—not because they were sinful people, though. They had to wear torn clothes. They had to keep their hair unkempt, if they had hair. They had to put a scarves around their faces or bandage the lower part of their faces. They would have to cry out "unclean, unclean," whenever they came near people in the community. Sometimes they even had to ring a little bell to alert others that an unclean person was coming near. They were total outcasts, but not sinful outcasts. That's an important distinction.

If you were Naaman in the Old Testament and you had leprosy, you were sort of doomed in society. If you were one of the 10 lepers that Christ met, you were the dregs of society, the disease in society, and you should stay away—you were quarantined from society. Can you imagine the deep psychological effect this had on people? The communal ramifications of their lives and lifestyle and the spiritual disorder of their lives have often been compared to our previous unfortunate treatment of LGBT persons. Some still erroneously believe LGBT persons don't belong in our community. Even the church's terminology is unfortunate, labeling LGBT people as intrinsically disordered or as having a grave depravity. Many people say we consign our LGBT sisters and brothers to a modern-day form of how lepers used to be treated.

Well, just look at these readings and see how God deals with a leper. How Jesus, who is God, deals with a leper. In the Old Testament, God's prophet Elisha tells Naaman to go plunge in the Jordan River seven times, and boom! Through the prophet, God cures Naaman of his leprosy. His flesh became like the flesh of a little child. God wanted Naaman to have flesh like a little child. Beautiful, beautiful!

Jesus, listening and hearing the 10 lepers cry out, cures all 10 of them and says not to go into the river, but go show yourself to the priest. They all go their way except one who doesn't even make it to the priest. One of them goes right back to Jesus and says thanks for enabling him or her to be clean, to be able to function once again in society—that leper gives thanks. As usual in some of Jesus's stories, that leper was not a Jew; that leper was a Samaritan and many Jews didn't like Samaritans. But God likes Jews, Samaritans, and every one of us. I think the point is that God, Jesus Christ, is calling us to live in community with one another. For example, Jerusalem is not a great city because of a port or an industry; it's only great because of God's presence in Jerusalem. There are Jews, Muslims, and Christians—all are called to be in community with one another, and live together with one another, and love one another.

I think that's what God is calling us to do; to live, love, forgive, and be good for one another in community. The Republicans, the Democrats, and the Tea Party are called to live in community and work in community to love, forgive, and contribute. You can say the same thing about the community of Christian churches. It's not just "we are right, and you are wrong," but we need to live in community with one another. Finally, it includes our family, our friends, our fellow parishioners and neighbors: we're called to live in community.

That's the will of God; that's the vision of Jesus. I think that's why God in the Old Testament and Jesus in the New Testament chose lepers who had been ostracized and God says "I want to bring them back. Come join the community, the Kingdom of God." We might not see lepers around now, but we have others that surely must feel like lepers when we ostracize them, shun them, shut them out from our parishes and our hearts, our communities and our networks— those with whom we do not even try to live in community. And so, we ask ourselves, are we part of the problem or part of the solution?

Gracious God, help me be part of the solution. Give me the grace, the vision, the insight to know how to be part of the solution that you have in mind.

WHAT IS YOUR SPIRITUALITY?

Acts 13:14, 43–52
Rv 7:9, 14–17
Jn 10:27–30

In today's Gospel, Jesus says, "My sheep hear my voice." In order to belong to Jesus, to follow him, we must hear him. When acts of violence and hatred occur in this world today, we must know that the perpetrators are not listening to Jesus.

Listening to God and Jesus in our hearts is basically our spirituality. Jesus says, "Listen to me, you are one of my sheep, and my sheep hear my voice."

You and I have to ask ourselves, "Why do I do what I do? To whom do I listen?"

What is your spirituality? As for me, I try to listen to the words, the life, and the message of Jesus in my life every day.

Your spirituality is really about to whom you listen, what ideas you listen to, and what you try to do in your life.

Pope Francis listens to Jesus. He listens only to Jesus. If he would not have listened to Jesus, he would never have done what he did; he would never have led the life that he lives. He developed his lifestyle and insights by listening to Jesus, and he decided to live accordingly.

That has been my hope and my focus for my whole life: listen to Jesus. I ask you to do the exact same thing: listen to Jesus.

When we listen to Jesus, we develop our own spirituality. Ask yourself questions like these. To whom do I listen? What leads me? What drives me? What gives me insight? Why do I do what I want to do? What is my life all about? What is God calling me to do?

Do you ask yourself these questions? How should I act? Where should I go? With whom should I be? Answering these questions while listening to Jesus in your heart is working on your salvation. It gives meaning to life.

Jesus says, "My sheep hear my voice." What do you hear in your heart? Do you follow your heart? That's your spirituality.

So, if you have difficulty hearing the voice of Jesus, take some time out, be quiet, settle down, and remove yourself from daily activity. It helps to have peace and quiet when listening to the voice of Jesus inside you.

Gracious God, help me listen to the voice of Jesus. Help me be quiet and settle my mind so that I can hear his voice.

The Rest of the Story

1 Mc 7:2, 9–14
2 Thes 2:16–3:5
Lk 20:27–38

I am borrowing from the sayings of Paul Harvey, a popular radio commentator, who always ended his broadcast with the words "that was the rest of the story."

From the scriptural readings for today's homily, we find that the focus is on the resurrection of the body. In the Second Book of Maccabees, we are told about seven brothers who are being tortured and killed by a king who is asking them to violate sacred laws handed to them by their ancestors, the Jews. These men all submit to death with statements that the king of this world will raise us up to live forever. They are proclaiming their belief in their God and in his plan that they will each be resurrected to be with him. They see this resurrection as the rest of the story for each of them.

In Luke, Jesus is asked by the Sadducees, a group that denies the resurrection, what happens after we die? What is the rest of the story? Jesus explains to them the reality of the resurrection of the body.

Jesus explains to them that we are all going to rise from the dead, and there is a resurrection of the body. There will be a resurrection of your body. How that body will look is not explained. I believe that our new condition is going to be some combination of our spirit and our soul connected with a material body.

Even at the time of Jesus, when he was speaking, Jesus did not reveal details about the resurrection. We are aware that the body we now have will die. But life is not ended; it is changed.

According to our faith and belief, the body will rise again somehow, some way, and look somewhat different.

So, the rest of the story for us is that there will be a resurrection. We, however, are not provided with much detail about that resurrection. After Christ died and rose again, he had a new body. His same spirit, Jesus, was connected with the new material body. He appeared here and there and was not recognized by his followers. He entered rooms when the doors were all locked.

We are left guessing about the actual reality of life after the resurrection. We must guess about the details. We should remember in our guessing that the sky is the limit.

Gracious God, help me make a priority of living in harmony with you so that we can share the rest of the story together.

PLATO, EINSTEIN, AND JESUS

Is 6:1–2, 3–8
1 Cor 15:1–11
Lk 5:1–11

In today's Gospel, Peter listens to Jesus. (This is not always the case.) He listens to Jesus and receives an abundance of fish in his nets.

I recently read an article in the paper identifying some little sayings of great people. There was one by Plato: "When there is an income tax, the just will pay more than the unjust;" another by Aristotle: "When there is no middle class, and the poor greatly exceed in number, troubles arise, and the state soon comes to an end;" another perhaps by Native Americans: "Treat the earth well; it was not given to you by your parents, it was loaned to you by your children;" another by Einstein: "Only two things are infinite—the universe and human stupidity . . . I am not sure about the former;" and finally a quote attributed to Napoleon, "And in the end, it is religion that keeps the poor from murdering the rich."

All of this wisdom is from great people giving great insights, and the point is, do we listen? At some time, we all find ourselves in over our heads and beyond our power to control what is happening. Do we then listen to great people? Do we follow their wisdom, or do we just listen and disregard them and do it our way?

Peter, in this great incident of the miraculous catch of fish, listens to the command of Jesus and does it Jesus's way. Peter says to Jesus,

"Master, we have worked all night and have caught nothing, but at your command, I will lower the nets."

As Jesus made Peter and the apostles "fishers of men," he also calls us to listen to him and follow him. And while we may have struggles, work hard and feel our efforts are fruitless, we need to keep going and listen to Jesus and not be afraid. For just as sure as dawn follows night, success will follow in our lives.

Now is the time to meditate on the wisdom that comes from Jesus. What does he command us to be and to do? His insights are much greater than all those of Plato, or Einstein.

Gracious God, give me open ears to hear the message of Jesus and follow him.

WE ARE CALLED TO
READ AND MEDITATE
ON SCRIPTURE

Jer 1:4–5,17–19
1 Cor 12:31–13:13
Lk 4:21–30

The Gospel today begins with Jesus in Nazareth where he grew up. He is now an adult and goes into the synagogue and reads the Old Testament scripture according to Jeremiah.

While many "spoke highly of him and were amazed at the gracious words that came from his mouth," a good number of those in the audience, who had known him as a young man, wanted to know from him, "Who do you think you are?"

This becomes a personal issue for me. I have two brothers, Dick and Paul. I believe that since they are both deceased, they are in heaven. But often, after I was ordained, we would have discussions. They would ask me, "Who do you think you are?" They did not appreciate their belief that I was preaching to them.

I must tell you that I never have felt any better or smarter than they were. I am here talking about the power and insights of Jesus. I do not have power; Jesus has the power. The words and insights of Jesus are his power in my life; it comes from him, not me.

I have chosen to pursue the priesthood and therefore have had an amazing education in theology. I have studied Karl Rahner, considered probably the greatest theologian in the last one hundred years. I studied in Innsbruck, Austria.

In my studies, we read the scriptures; we discussed what true spirituality really is. In order to study in Innsbruck, I left behind my family, my familiar surroundings, and I was required to learn languages such as German and Latin. It had its difficulties. In retrospect, it was the greatest blessing in my life. I did not become better than other people, or necessarily holier than others, but I gained amazing insights. I try to offer them to others through reading, absorbing, and sharing my understanding of the scriptures.

It is in the reading of the scriptures that I have found true holiness. You have been called to read the scriptures; by doing so, you will also find insights into Jesus. You will find, as referenced in scripture, the amazing and great and gracious words that come from the mouth of Jesus. You will learn how to live better and happier and holier lives. Scripture says that you have been called. God "knew you in the womb." Listen to my Word, says God, take out time to pray and say, "What would Jesus do?"

Don't ever think that the power and greatness of scripture is coming from you. It is coming from God. It is a gift because of his love.

Jesus performed some miracles during his ministry here on earth. The greatest miracle is his sacrifice for us. The transforming of self through reading and understanding scripture is our path to receiving the complete miracle that Jesus offers.

Paul tells us in Corinthians that we must strive for the greatest spiritual gifts. Through the scriptures we learn that love is the greatest of all Christian acts. Jesus demonstrated that in his life and death.

Gracious God, help me love like you love. That's all. Amen.

Season Evergreen

Jer 33:14–16
1 Thes 3:12–4:2
Lk 21:25–28, 34–36

This is the beginning of the liturgical year as we prepare for Christmas. We are celebrating the coming of the Messiah, as a baby, the presence of the Messiah in the world during his life, and the future coming of the Messiah at the end of time.

The Christmas season offers the first manifestation of Christ in the liturgical year through his birth. Here he becomes a real human. This is experienced by those close to him in Bethlehem. The second event further manifesting Christ is the coming of the Magi to witness his birth and proclaim him to the greater world. Next, he is further manifested through his baptism by John in the Jordan River, where the announcement that Christ is from God is made. Then his manifestation as a worker of miracles occurs at the wedding in Cana of Galilee, when he turns 150 gallons of water to wine.

The first reading from Jeremiah is about the coming of Jesus Christ. We enter into the celebration of this new beginning through the symbols present in the lighting of the Advent wreath. The symbols are simple, but I never tire of meditating on them. The wreath is a "circle A circle has no beginning and no end. The Messiah, God, also has no beginning and no end. When we join with God, although we have had a beginning, we will have no end. We will be one with God forever.

The fact that the wreath is made from evergreen foliage is symbolic of the truth that God is the Alpha and the Omega, and this Messiah has everlasting life. God is always and forever green.

The wreath is decorated with four candles. Each candle represents one of the four weeks of Advent. Three of the candles are purple, reminding us of the penitential aspect of the Advent season. The candle representing the third week is pink. This candle is lit on Gaudete Sunday, reminding us of the coming end of Advent and the joy of Christmas ahead.

The reading from Luke changes focus from the joy of the arrival of Christ in the world, as described by Jeremiah, to the frightful condition of the world both then and now. Luke is describing an end-of-time situation. In our world today, we are witnessing so much that is frightening. Individuals are destroying lives of others and even their own lives through terrorist activity. These violent people do not seem to love themselves and therefore must not be able to love others. Jesus calls us to love ourselves and thereby to love our neighbor as ourselves.

So, on this first Sunday of Advent, we can appreciate the beginning of the liturgical year and be enlightened by the beauty of the Advent wreath. We can prepare for the manifestations of Jesus Christ throughout the liturgical year and understand that there is so much work to be done within ourselves and in the world to prepare for the coming of the Messiah at the end of time.

Gracious God, help me to be open to your love, receive it with an open heart, and spread it generously, like you do.

Am I Humble? Are You Humble?

Sir 3:17–18, 20, 28–29
Heb 12:18–19, 22–24
Lk 14:1, 7–14

Let's look at the banquet: what is done, why these people go, how they pull it off, and what Christ is trying to say about humility and pride.

They go to the banquet—and they were invited—so they choose a place of honor, then they get kicked out of the place of honor, and they're humiliated. They go in with pride and they wind up being humiliated. Well, I think that's true. Pride and humility in religion, and true religion or false religion, I think, are terribly related. For example, in this situation, Christ is saying, "We are called to be humble before God and do the will of God as opposed to just my will and feeding my pride."

That is, I think, very interesting in today's world relative to religion: true and false religion. Here in the Gospel, Christ is talking about pride and humility—and even the first reading speaks of it, from the priest or the book of Sirach. The person of God is the humble person as the priest Sirach says, "My child, conduct your affairs with humility." Then he goes on to say that the more you humble yourself, the greater you are. Then finally, "Humble yourself and you will find favor with God."

I think our religion is trying to convey the same thing. You could go to that wedding reception and go to the lowest place only so that you would be placed up higher and you would be above all the other people there, because the bride and the groom bring you to the table of honor. You could do that only so that you'd be given a better place. That intent is different from the intent in the Gospel reading. You can also do the exact same thing with religion.

There's true religion and there's false religion. This is true in Roman Catholicism and Islam. Oh, we could quickly point to the Islamic faith and say, "It's a religion of violence!" It really isn't; it's a religion of submitting to God, which is humiliating and humbling and a true religion.

Some people take that religion and they just take a little bit out of it or a parcel out of it or a sentence out of it or an idea out of it, and they make that the important part of that religion. I think that's terribly, terribly false.

Islam was founded by Muhammad in the seventh century, and we can see that it is really about submitting to the will of God and not about killing the infidel. Truly, it is good religion to submit to the will of God.

We can say the exact same thing about Roman Catholicism. Roman Catholicism is trying to project the will of Jesus, the will of the Father—humility, forgiveness, love, all of these—and we do, but we do not do it perfectly. There is a lot of false religion in many of our concepts of Roman Catholicism. I don't have time to pull out that list and keep harping on that, but just think for yourself and you'll figure out what I mean.

Are we as clear in judging some of our false concepts of the will of God? Do you spend some time doing that? I certainly think it would not be wasted time. Oh, we can be proud that we have the revelation of Jesus Christ, and we are rightly proud. We claim it's the fullest revelation. But God revealed himself to the Jewish people also. God revealed himself to Muhammad and the people of the Eastern world.

It's so easy to do things and do them with false religion or to do them with pride and not with humility.

Think, pray, and ask yourself if all these factors come together with the Kingdom of God at the banquet, the wedding banquet. Do I see every sister and brother as a child of God?

IF THE CHURCH
WOULD ONLY . . .

Gn 15:5–12, 17–18
Phil 3:17–4:1
Lk 9:28–36

This Gospel tells us about the Transfiguration of Jesus on Mount Tabor. Reflecting on this passage brings back many happy memories for me. When I went on my first sabbatical, I lived in Rome for three months. Before returning home, I was able to go to the Holy Land with 36 other priests.

At each of the many sites in the Holy Land, we celebrated Mass together and then went our separate ways to reflect and pray about that site. I was chosen to deliver the homily at the site of the Transfiguration. It was an experience that has been engraved on my heart.

So many questions arise from this Gospel passage: Why Peter, James, and John? Why Moses and Elijah? Why three tents? Why the dazzling white? And this voice—what does that really mean? I am not sure about all that, but I do know that what moved me was the voice that came out of the cloud, the Father saying this about Jesus: "This is my chosen Son; listen to Him."

What impacted me the most are those words: "Listen to Him."

When Pope Benedict XVI announced his resignation, many people were excited and were saying, "Well, now is the chance, now is the time, when the church is going to change. Won't it be wonderful?" Well, I had my doubts because I really believe that change doesn't come from the top down, but it comes up from the grassroots. Yes, I was excited about a new pope, but what I am most excited about is listening to Jesus.

For years now, many have been asking, "When are we going to have female priests?" And priests are asking, "When will we be able to get married?" These are important questions but, wow, they are not the most important. The most important thing is to listen to Jesus. I must listen to Him in my life.

For years, we have been dealing with corruption in the church. Look at all those priest abusers. Not just the criminal sinfulness of that, but the cover-up connected with it. That's got to change.

The most important thing—whether you're the pope, the bishop, Father Larry, or you—the most important thing is to listen to Christ, listen to Him.

I'm bringing up all these complaints that we have. People who say, "I'm tired of the church telling me, or my bishop telling me how to vote. That's my responsibility. Don't tell me how to vote or don't try to just coax me into it or tell me that if I have a conscience, I've got to vote this way." Well, that's not the most important thing. The most important thing is to listen to Jesus.

"This is my Beloved Son; listen to Him."

We don't do it too much anymore, but it used to be that every time you went to church, it was money, money, money. Buy this raffle ticket, buy this or give more—we need help in the school. They need more money, money, money. Money is important. But the most important thing is Jesus; listen to Him.

Since I've been a priest—for many years—the conservatives have been warring against the liberals and the liberals have been warring against the conservatives. Each side says, "If we were all this way, it would be a whole new church. And I guarantee you a better church because this is unconservative or unliberal, and this is the way the church ought to be."

Not true. It takes liberals and conservative in the church. However, for anything to change for the better, we need to listen to Christ. "This is my beloved Son; listen to Him."

Each one of us can pick our own statement: If only the church would _____ (you fill in the blank), it would be better.

Baloney! The church needs to listen to the basic message of Jesus Christ. We can't go wrong if we do that. We can't go wrong.

Take out the New Testament during Lent. Take time for prayer. Settle down and "waste" some time in silence and listen to Jesus Christ. He is the Son of the Father. He is the message to the world! Nothing but the message of Jesus really matters.

Gracious God, help me to listen to Jesus. Give me wisdom so I can do my part to accomplish what is mine to do.

ARE YOU SAVED?

Is 66:18–21
Heb 15:5–7, 11–13
Lk 13:22–30

This weekend, we wrap up the Olympics, and I think it has something to do with the Gospel reading. I call this, "Jesus, The Great Olympic Coach." This weekend, only a few will get the gold and silver and bronze medals. All of those athletes have been training for years and only a few get the medals and very, very few are disqualified.

Jesus was sent by God, His Father, who I like to say is, "The great Olympic coach." People of all countries, speaking all languages, participate in the Olympics, and they have experienced blood, sweat, and tears for many years: four years, eight years, twelve years, in preparation for it. With Jesus, the great Olympic coach, all who participate are winners. All who take part in the Olympics, all those athletes from all over the world, they are winners.

Let's look at the Gospel. Someone—let's just say an Olympian or an athlete—asked Jesus Christ, "Will only a few be saved or only a few win the medals?" Jesus says this, "Strive to do your best. Many have already tried but did not make it. Only a few will get the medals." What Jesus said in the Gospel is, "Strive to enter through the narrow gate, for I tell you, many will attempt to enter but will not be strong enough." With Jesus and the God of the Old Testament, Yahweh, and really even our church doctrine, all are saved.

Look at that first sentence in Isaiah 66. It says, "Thus says the Lord, 'I know their works and their thoughts, and I come to gather nations of every language and they shall come and see my glory.'"

Jesus, in our doctrine of the incarnation, has become a man, and Jesus, sent by the Father, has come and saved us all. All creation won gold! All those who participate in creation become winners and they get the medals and all creation is saved. Every person is saved, but there's a problem; some have the possibility of disqualifying themselves and then, through their own free will, they are not saved. That's the only way that you cannot be saved.

The question has come up since the time of the apostles: "Today, how many are saved?" All, some, few, most? Ten percent, 95 percent? I don't absolutely know, but I remember, as a child, I used to think, "Roman Catholics are saved, and I'm not too sure about everybody else." Then, as a seminarian and a theologian, I began to realize how broad this incarnation and salvation is through Jesus Christ. I liked this idea. In the early church, it was heresy. In Latin, the concept was called *pauci electi*—only a few are saved. The church has since condemned this.

Some religions, like the Jehovah's Witnesses, believe that only 144,000 are saved from each tribe. We read it in the Book of Revelation: 144,000 saved. Often, I think, we have the mentality that only a few will be saved. I really do not know the answer to that, but the older I become, the more I realize how wonderful God is, and God became one of us, and God wants to save us all.

In Richard McBrien's 1980 book, *Catholicism*, he noted that Jesus never said that people actually go to hell. Instead, Jesus addressed the possibility of not being saved. When people reject God, they choose an isolated existence. In this sense, hell (absolute isolation) is God yielding to our choice—a choice that rejects a life in community in favor of one lived in isolation.

Have you ever heard, "How can there be a God? I can't believe in a God who would send me to hell." I can't either. God doesn't. The only way we can get there is if we disqualify ourselves. That sounds pretty reasonable to me.

Is my image of God a realistic one? Is my relationship with God based on what Jesus revealed or upon irrational fear?

AM I A PROPHET?

Jer 38:4–6, 8–10
Heb 12:1–4
Lk 12:49–53

I used to not like this Gospel at all. It bothered me because of what Jesus said. He said, "I have come to set the earth on fire. Do you think that I've come to establish peace on earth? No, I tell you, but rather, division."

That always bothered me because I thought Jesus came to bring peace on earth, goodwill toward all. That's what it's all about, isn't it? Here, he says, "I didn't come to bring peace, but division." How does that fit into the world?

In our world, we have the division between the Republicans and Democrats. We have the 1 percent versus the rest, or the middle class versus those who are really on the bottom such as the homeless. There seems to be much division throughout the world. In Kentucky, our state motto is "United We Stand, Divided We Fall." Unity and division can be found in the church, in our nation, in our families, as well as in our personalities.

Well, what does Jesus really mean by his words in today's Gospel? Christ wants to set the world on fire. A common fire, that is. But how do we ever get the Democrats and Republicans together? How do we get the conservatives and liberals in the church together? Sometimes, how do we get Mom and Dad together?

If we don't, there is gridlock in government; there's fighting in families, mixed-up families; there's the conservatives and liberals in the church.

What about all this peace on earth, goodwill at Christmas? If you look at the earth right now and see the divisions and problems that we have, how are we going to achieve peace? You need a peaceful person, a peaceful attitude, a peaceful message to lead in the direction of unity and love and harmony and peace. That person, I think, is Jesus. For Jesus's message to take hold, there's going to be a lot of division. There's going to be a lot of sparks, much fire and heat and rugged discussions and arguments. Peace on earth, goodwill to men and women, doesn't come about easily.

Jesus wants this world, starting now, to be unified. He wants His message to set the world on fire. He wants to set your hearts on fire; it takes an awful lot of energy, though, to overcome evil. That's what He did. Look at the energy that He put in: suffering and dying on the cross. Look what all the prophets did, and what present-day prophets do. Look at all the good people in the world and look at us and what we do. That, I think is what Jesus talks about when He says, "I didn't come to bring peace but division." His division will lead to peace.

I now like the passage in today's Gospel, because I understand it a little bit better. It's up to you and me not to set out to cause division, but if we carry the message of Jesus, division will show itself. If our message is going to lead people in the direction of God, if it is headed toward peace on earth, goodwill to men and women, there is bound to be some division. I feel a lot more in tune with Jesus: to set the world on fire, to eradicate divisions and violence and wars, and really help bring about the Kingdom of God. What do you think about this reading? Do you like it? Do you understand it? I think I understand it a little bit more. How about you?

> *Gracious God, help me to build bridges and be a prophet that bring unity.*

Auschwitz vs. the Kingdom of God

Wis 18:6–9
Heb 11:1–2, 8–19
Lk 12:3–48

I don't know about you, but in the last few months, I've become sick and tired of the news. The Trayvon Martin case and trial and, more recently, the three young women who were kidnapped and held captive for over a decade and all those gory details. In this past week in the baseball world, there were the accusations of thirteen players using drugs. It just seems over and over again, there is weakness and sin. It was a bad week. But then I thought this is the opposite of the Kingdom of God, which is referred to in the Gospel.

I watch many different movies on Netflix. This week I started a new series called *Auschwitz*, about Hitler's concentration camps. There is a series of six one-hour movies; I've watched two. If you think the examples I gave earlier are terrible, this is overwhelmingly evil, depressing. I don't know if I can even watch the last four in the series! If that isn't the antithesis or the opposite of the Kingdom of God— what Hitler tried to do in the Third Reich, the third Empire, or the third kingdom—I don't know of anything that is worse.

We hear that six million Jews were killed, but in this first or second episode, it talked about over three million Russian soldiers were killed. Three more million! I started to think, how many million people died? I went to the internet, and I went to the World War II death count. I found two pages listing 30 different countries. Let me just tell you a couple: in the USSR, more than seven million civilians were killed. Then in their military, another 13 million. The deaths during World War II in the USSR totaled 21 million people. Germany civilian deaths were 3.8 million; military, 3.2 million. Seven million German people killed in that war!

More than 500,000 US military died in the Second World War. Civilian deaths? Zero. Thank God. In these 30 countries, the total number of people killed in World War II is more than 56 million people, according to the Hitler Historical Museum in 1999. If that isn't evil and the opposite of what Jesus Christ is trying to say, I don't know what is. The first reich or the first kingdom was Rome; the second kingdom or empire was the Byzantine Empire; and the third empire or *das dritte reich*, the third kingdom, was Hitler's. How evil, how opposite to the message of Jesus.

In the Gospel today, Jesus says, "Look, do not be afraid any longer, little flock, for your father is pleased to give you the kingdom."

That's what he's all about, and that's what we are all about—the Kingdom of God. Jesus, in the Gospel says, "For where your treasure is, there also will be your heart." Where is your heart? Where is your treasure? Where is my heart? Where is my treasure? The world has tried many kingdoms, and they won't ever work. The only real kingdom is the Kingdom of God, the only kingdom is the Kingdom of Jesus, and you and I are called to do our part in growing that kingdom and not give up and not stop—ever! Where your treasure is, there your heart will be. Isn't that what Jesus said when they asked Him, teach us how to pray?

"Our Father who art in heaven, hallowed be thy name, thy kingdom come. Thy will be done on earth as it is in heaven."

It's depressing in some ways, but also joyful and good news in another way, that you and I are called to participate in this Kingdom of God. I hope you feel it: not just feel the evils of the world but feel the joys of the relationship that we have with God. Feel the relationship that we're called to have with one another and feel the call that we are to be servants and to help establish this Kingdom of God. If you put your own heart in it, your treasure in it, you'll find great joy in every day until we get into the fullness of that kingdom that is in heaven.

What am I doing to promote the coming of the Kingdom of God?

COSMIC CHRIST

Wis 11:22–12:2
Thes 1:11–2:2
Lk 19:1–10

In today's homily, I am considering Jesus both from his historical presence in the Gospels, and his living presence throughout all time. The first Jesus is "historical" and the second is "cosmic."

In Luke, you have the historical Jesus walking with Zacchaeus. He calls to Zacchaeus to come down from the tree that Zacchaeus has climbed in an attempt to see Jesus. Zacchaeus was very short. Jesus says to Zacchaeus, "Come down quickly for today I must stay at your house." Jesus chooses to go to Zacchaeus's house. This happened 2000 years ago—historical Jesus.

Do you realize that today, in this time, Jesus is calling to us to come down from a tree and bring him into our homes? When you fully participate in the liturgy and communion at Mass, Jesus is saying to you, today I am going to stay in your house. Today I am going to eat with you. You are going to eat with me. You are going to be present with me. I am going to be present with you. We are going to be one at the table. This is the cosmic Jesus.

Zacchaeus, a sinner, was received by God, received by Jesus, and he abandoned his sins. This is the reason that Jesus went into his house. He loves the sinner and because of God's great love in Jesus, Zacchaeus changes. The tax collector changes for the better.

Zacchaeus, who had been greedy and dishonest in his dealings with his fellow humans, said, Lord, I will give to the poor. He also says that anyone whom he had cheated in the past, he would repay four times the amount he gained through his cheating. Salvation had come to Zacchaeus's house.

This is why we go back and receive Christ and talk and listen to Christ at communion time. This is why we expose this Sacred Host in benediction and fall down on our knees and adore Christ. If you understand this, that God is in his creation and that God is in Jesus who became one of us through the incarnation, then you must know that we are united with the historical Christ and we are united with the cosmic Christ. They are one and the same.

Gracious God, help me hear Jesus calling me and help me respond eagerly.

THE MESSIAH, CHRISTOS, JESUS

Bar 5:1–9
Phil 1:4–6, 8–11
Lk 3:1–6

While meditating on today's readings, in which Baruch describes a future paradise, and Luke calls for repentance and preparing a way for the Lord, I began thinking about the state of the world in which we live. As far as I can understand, the world is now and always has been messed up. Throughout all recorded history, this has been true. Stories in scripture attempt to explain this problem: Old Testament stories about Adam and Eve and the serpent in the garden, the story about the brothers Cain and Abel, the story about Noah and the Great Flood. These stories tell us that what God made, his creation, was initially good. What happened to God's creation, its decline, was our fault.

Throughout Old Testament history, many great leaders came forth to repair the damage that had occurred to God's creation. Abraham led the Jewish people at about 1850 BC and Moses came forward in 1250 BC. The prophets were active from 1000 BC–500 BC. Kings were influenced and led by God.

None of these people could make the world good, ordered, or redeemed. This could only occur with divine help. We have always needed and continue to need a Savior and Messiah. Even John the Baptist, the greatest among men and women, could not save us. He described himself as "a voice of one crying in the desert." He cries out, "Prepare the way of the Lord, make straight his way." John was telling everyone that the Messiah was coming.

We need divine help to save the world. We need a Messiah; we need Jesus the Messiah, Jesus the Christos, Jesus Christ. Matthew says in chapter 1:21 that Yahweh will save his people from their sins. The term *Yahweh* embraces the title Jesus, Christos, Messiah. John knew that salvation was coming through the person of Jesus Christ. He was teaching this and telling us to prepare for the beautiful coming of Christ.

This preparation, however, is not a pleasant emotional movement. In Luke, chapter 12:49, Jesus says that he has not come to establish peace on earth, but that he has come to "set the earth on fire, and how I wish it were already burning."

To find a direction to help us prepare for the future coming of Christ, I share this analogy. We must think of ourselves and all others as dirty laundry. We were created good, pure, and white, but we have become dirty clothes. We have been dirtied by evil. The evil described in Genesis and the story of the Garden of Eden is actively at work in the world.

Jesus—or God—is like a washing machine and water and soap. Jesus wants us to climb into that washer, let it tumble for 20 minutes, 20 years, 20 millennia to get us pure white and clean. Then into the dryer we go. You can think of the fabric softener with a lovely fragrance as the Holy Spirit freshening and giving us a wonderful smell. All of us on planet earth need to be purified. Then we will be prepared for the return of Christ.

It seems that the return of Christ is slow in coming, but it's as certain as your belief in God that the Messiah has come, that the Messiah is here, and the Messiah will come again. That is the meaning of the Advent season.

Gracious God, help me be a positive force in the world to help restore beauty and grandeur.

Prodigal Son

Jos 5:9–12
2 Cor 5:17–21
Lk 15:1–3, 11–32

This rather long passage deals with the prodigal son. Some people prefer to call it the Gospel of the prodigal father. This is the story of two sons—one good, one bad—and a very good father.

My father, Stan, had five children: one son Paul, with his first wife, then two daughters and two sons (Dick and me) with his second wife, my mother.

Dick was about two and a half years older than me. Being much stronger, he could easily whip me. This led to a lot of sibling rivalry. Dick was strong, but I was clever. One day we were playing blind-man's bluff upstairs. I tied the blind over Dick's eyes and as I led him around, I explained, "Now you are going into your bedroom, now into our sister's bedroom, the bathroom, our parent's room." This last statement was not true. I had led him to the stairwell and told him to take one giant step for humankind. He went tumbling down the stairs and almost killed himself. My father was so angry, he almost killed me! Two sons, Dick and Larry. We were both good and both bad. Like the sons in the Gospel.

In this classic Gospel story (considered the finest short story in the New Testament) we see the wild first son blow the money he got from his estate or his father on prostitutes and wild living. Then he comes to his senses and returns home. His father embraces him with open arms.

The second son, who is a goody-two-shoes, gets upset that his father welcomed his brother back. This father loved both sons. He was a great father. This story reminds us of God the Father's love for each of us. Always! Infinitely! Always ready to forgive.

Like the father in the Gospel. Let's have a big party. "He's back! He's come home! He's shaping up! He's wonderful. Put a ring on him. Put a coat or robe on him. Let's cut the fattened calf."

The other son was good, too. He worked hard. That father was a super-duper, first-class father. Those two sons were like Dick and Larry. I might have been the more evil one because I'm sure I had the police at the door more than anyone else in the family. I don't remember Dick or Paul ever having the police at the front door.

We see that God's love is so good. It's even better than the love of this father. I think over many years the church has made God an angry man; a God who really wants us to shape up. I'm sorry, folks; that's not God. God loves you before you change, when you change, when you sin, and if you don't change. God totally loves you.

Here's the clincher! God loves you so much that if you ever realize that, you will change. God loves us when we sin. God wants to forgive us. God wants us to change, but God is not waiting for us to change before he loves us.

The second son would not go into the party. He says, "This son of yours did all these things." He would not go into the party. He continues, "All these years I served you, and not once did I disobey your orders, and yet you never even gave me a young goat to feast on with my friends. But when your son returns who swallowed up your property with prostitutes, for him you slaughtered the fattened calf."

Here's a little something about my father. My father loved when I went to the seminary. I would come home for Thanksgiving, Christmas, or other occasions, and my father would ask, "Larry, what would you like for supper?" My sister Nancy would get really upset with my father, and say, "I'm here all the time and you never ask me what I want for supper. He comes back from the seminary and you ask him 'What do you want for supper?'"

The lessons in this story not only apply to two sons. They apply to brothers and sisters, husbands and wives, moms and dads. God loves us infinitely. God loves us even when we are not good. The rain comes down on the just and the unjust. The love of God is on the just and the unjust; on the kind and the unkind. We're the ones who have the problem. We need to change, and to realize how much God loves us. If you realize that, you are going to love yourself. You're going to be happy with yourself. You will be happy.

> *Take some time to realize how much you are loved; despite whatever you have done or left undone, realize how deeply you are loved by God. Then go and be happy!*

HURLING STONES
IS NOT MERCY

Is 43:16–21
Phil 3:8–14
Jn 8:1–11

In Jesus's time, stoning was a means of capital punishment. It was apparently not only permitted, but required, under the Mosaic Law.

The Pharisees brought a woman to Jesus while he was teaching in the temple. She had been caught in adultery. They made her stand in the middle of them all while those Pharisees told Jesus that this woman should be stoned to death under the law.

Jesus, in his great wisdom, dispersed the accusers by asking them, "Which of you are without sin?"

Scripture tells us that at that moment in history, terrible, violent acts were being committed in the name of religion. Sadly, is not much different today, maybe it is even worse.

In the Middle East, religious zealots are stoning their fellow humans, and more extreme groups are doing far more horrible things.

Jesus Christ, two thousand years ago, brought about an amazing new insight: as the Jewish crowd was about to stone a woman to death, he said, "Let the person without sin throw the first stone." They all left.

Jesus asked the woman, "Where are your accusers? They did not condemn, nor will I. Go and sin no more."

Jesus brought a fresh insight. Pope Francis is also bringing fresh insights. Pope Francis is asking us to look at Jesus and his mercy in a new way.

While we, as a country, do not permit stoning, we do allow for lawful killing through capital punishment. We also stone people to death with the stones of attitudes, biases, prejudices, words, innuendo, and the cowardice that hides judgment behind the guise of being a "good" Catholic or Christian.

Jesus looks to mercy, not killing or hurling stones. What a more holy and beautiful world it would be if all forms of taking human life or destroying the spirit of a brother or sister—especially by Pharisaical judgment—were understood to be contrary to the Gospel.

Jesus is a genius!

How do I understand and live a life of mercy and love? How can I be more like Jesus when I am tempted to hurl a stone and condemn a sister or a brother?

CRASHING OR GENTLY, IT IS THE SPIRIT

Gn 11:1–9
Acts 2:1–11
Jn 14:15–16, 23–26

In Genesis, we read about the Tower of Babel. This structure was built in order to create disunity among the people who were attempting to build a way to access heaven. They must have been unaware of the evil involved in that act, or maybe they just didn't care.

This disunity operates in our world today, as it did in the time of Babel. Today eastern and western countries are in disunity; first world, second world and third world countries are in conflict.

Our government is constantly in disunity at both the federal and state levels. Families can often be disunited. Sometimes there is disunity within us.

Then there is this great gift of the coming of the Holy Spirit at Pentecost. The Holy Spirit is with us to help us become what we are called to become. The Spirit comes to remove the disunity that prevents us from coming together in the oneness God has planned for us.

Jesus and the Holy Spirit provide the answer to all disunity. Jesus, on Easter Sunday evening, enters the upper room when the doors were locked, and says, "Peace be with you." He comes to bring peace into the world. He says to the disciples, "Receive the Holy Spirit, whose sins you forgive are forgiven."

Jesus is calling us to forgive each other, ourselves, other countries, every brother and sister. We are called to forgive every person who sins against us.

The Holy Spirit came upon the early church at Pentecost in the form of a mighty wind, tongues of fire, and a loud noise.

The Holy Spirit comes into our hearts and minds through baptism, confirmation, and prayer. The Spirit comes to all of us—sacramentally, sometimes subtly, sometimes crashing into our lives. Do I listen to Jesus and the Holy Spirit?

In a reading from the *Liturgy of the Hours* for Pentecost Sunday is this prayer: "Teach us, good Lord, to serve the needs of others, help us to give and not to count the cost, unite us all for we are born as brothers and sisters; defeat our Babel with your Pentecost."

How am I living the Spirit's call to promote unity? Am I aware of the Spirit's promptings in my imagination, mind, heart, soul?

EASTER SUNDAY

Acts 10:34a, 37–41
Col 3:1–4
Jn 20:1–9

All during Holy Week, we have been focusing on the journey of Christ to his death on the cross. We must experience physical death just as Jesus did. Death comes to each one of us; it cuts us down and turns our flesh into dust and ashes. Death is part of life.

But now we read about this beautiful Easter experience and we are brought into Christ's new life and filled with hope because of new insight.

In the Acts of the Apostles, we are told, "God raised Jesus on the third day." Christ's resurrection destroyed death, broke the chain of death. We now have new life, new light, and a new insight.

In the Gospel, Mary of Magdala and two disciples, Peter and John, find an empty tomb. Later that same night, while his followers were all gathered, the resurrected Jesus appears to them. And, more than that, there is an empty tomb!

The empty tomb and the resurrected Jesus transcend all else. After his resurrection, Jesus appears many times. He makes his presence felt, known, experienced.

Jesus is light. The beauty of a sunrise Easter liturgy is that we can experience the rising of the sun during the Mass as it represents the amazingly glorious light that Jesus has brought into the world.

Sometimes there are cloudy skies. Sometimes our lives are clouded by problems. Jesus, the light, is always there.

He is alive with a new body. He will change us by giving us a new and resurrected body; a body that will never die, that will always be with Him.

Jesus is transformed with a new resurrected body, and Jesus will transform us by giving us a new and resurrected body.

Jesus gives us new life, new light, forever. We will be one with the light, forever. Indeed, the greatest feast that we have is this Easter feast that lasts for eternity!

How can I communicate the joy of this beautiful Easter experience to others to whom Christ's joy has not yet come?

SUFFERING

Ex 3:1–15
1 Cor 10:1–6, 10–12
Lk 13:1–9

How do we understand the presence of so much suffering in the world?

Suffering is addressed when, in Exodus, we see God's compassion toward the Israelites. The Israelites are suffering in Egypt under the control of the Pharaoh. God is preparing to send Moses to release them from that suffering.

The Jewish people, even after being liberated from Egypt and the Pharaoh, continue to face hardships during their time in the desert. Did they understand why they had to suffer and die in the desert?

In Luke's Gospel, Jesus is questioned regarding why people must suffer. He was asked why 18 people had to die when a tower fell on them.

The questioners wanted to know if those people had died because they had sinned. Jesus, addressing their question, asked them if they believed that those 18 people were guiltier of sin than any other person. If they did believe that, Jesus told them that they were wrong.

He then added this warning, "But unless you repent, you will perish as they did."

Jesus also offers the parable of the fig tree that was not bearing fruit. He points out that, while the landlord would give the tree a little more time to bear fruit, and would help it along with fertilizer and care, eventually, if the tree continued to bear no fruit, it would be chopped down.

And then we have Job. He was subject to unjust suffering. Unjust suffering is our universal experience on earth. Job remained faithful to God throughout his suffering. He said, "I know I have a living defender. He will raise me up at last. He will set me close to Him, and from my flesh I shall look on God." Job never gave up.

Jesus also faced his suffering with faith. He asked God, "Why have you forsaken me?" But Jesus lived to do the will of God. He forgave his persecutors.

We may not ever understand the value of or the need for suffering until we pass from this world. But God understood why the Jewish people, Job, and Jesus were asked to endure suffering. This is where our faith that God has a purpose is essential; we need to understand the message of Jesus: we need to trust in God even when we don't understand.

Do I view my personal suffering as a way that brings me closer to God?

ACKNOWLEDGMENTS

Without the following people, this book would not be in your hands. I am deeply grateful to these women and men of great faith, listed in alphabetical order:

- Whit DuPree

- Sr. Clara Fehringer, OSU

- Gerri Hine

- Ken Martin

- Margie Ralph

- Ann Stiene-Martin

- Bishop John Stowe, OFM Conv.

- Stan "JR" Zerkowski

- Trustees of the Thomas Merton Legacy Trust for permission to use Merton's Prayer

- The 92 generous benefactors who subsidized the publication of this book and believed in the dream

None of the aforementioned received any remuneration, gratuity, or any form of compensation for assistance with this book.